The 31 Day Family Dare

A Daily Dialog About Core Values

By

Greg C. Gunn

ISBN-13: 978-1492958291

Published

By

BeyondYourManuscript.com

Your Family Name

Your Family

Vision Statement

_____

_____

_____

_____

_____

_____

_____

_____

Your Family

Mission Statement

_____

_____

_____

_____

_____

_____

_____

_____

_____

_____

_____

_____

_____

_____

_____

_____

The 31 Day Family Dare
A Daily Dialog About Core Values

INSTRUCTIONS: "I dare you to..."

Age 1-6 – Pray a prayer over your children each evening. See examples below each value.

Age 7-13 – Each morning write the value on a 3x5 note card for each child. Ask them to learn the definition during the day and write it on the card. At the end of the day discuss the value and how it applies to your family.

Age 14 & up - Text (with cell phone) each day's value to each family member. Have a group text dialog throughout the day discussing the value and living it out.

Your goal is to make sure each family member understands the meaning of the word and how it applies in your family's daily culture. Text the prayer to your kids who have cell phones.

"I dare you! This will change your family!" --- Greg Gunn

Notes: _____

_____

_____

_____

_____

_____

_____

_____

_____

_____

_____

_____

_____

_____

BELONGING

It is important that each member of your family feel that they are loved, that they belong and that they matter. Being a cohesive family could mean that you spend every spare minute together doing family activities but keep in mind that everyone is different. Creating a strong family unit is great but each person should be allowed the space and freedom to explore the activities they think they may enjoy. People are more courageous and more willing to take chances if they know they have a safe place to come back to when things don't quite work out. Coming together for special occasions and holidays and just spending time together as a family is what helps build that sense of belonging.

"I pray _"child"_ will always feel a special part of our family. I ask you to help him/her always make their sibling feel loved and important to the family...
...In Jesus name, Amen."

Day 1

Notes: _____

_____

_____

_____

_____

_____

_____

_____

_____

_____

_____

_____

_____

_____

FLEXIBILITY

I'm all for order, schedules and structure in my family to help maintain some level of sanity. But too much structure and the unwillingness to give a little can result in a lot of unhappiness and resentment. The more flexibility you have in decision-making, for example, the happier your family will be for it. Imagine one member of the family always thinking they are right and enforcing their way of doing things. This certainly wouldn't lead to much happiness within the family unit.

"I pray *"child"* may grow in the love and grace toward their family members. I ask you make him/her flexible when the challenges of life come...   ...In Jesus name, Amen"

Day 2

Notes: _____

_____

_____

_____

_____

_____

_____

_____

_____

_____

_____

_____

_____

MARGIN

Craig Groeschel said, "Ministry happens in the margins of life!" We are going to be a family who makes sure we have margin in our time and money. We will have time in our lives every day, every week and every month where we can be available to be good Samaritans to people who cross our path. The good Samaritan had the time and the money to help! Relationship is built in the margins of life.

"I pray _"child"_ will always know that people are more important than things, money or time. Help him/her have a servants heart toward other people all of the time...   ...In Jesus name, Amen."

Day 3

Notes: _____

_____

_____

_____

_____

_____

_____

_____

_____

_____

_____

_____

_____

Relationships

Say it: "It's all about RELATIONSHIPS!"
Teenagers don't rebel against authority, they rebel against a lack of relationship! How do you improve any relationship? Spend conflict-free time together. It's true, the more time you spend together, the relationship goes up and the less time, it goes down. Make sure you are spending time alone with your spouse. Do fun things together and talk about dreams and ideas.

"I pray _"child"_ will learn the importance of having a great relationship with God, Dad, Mom, Siblings, Extended Family & Future Spouse...   ...In Jesus name, Amen."

Day 4

Notes: _____

_____

_____

_____

_____

_____

_____

_____

_____

_____

_____

_____

_____

GENEROSITY

2 Corinthians 9:8,9 "And God is able to bless you abundantly, so that in all things at all times, having all that you need, you will abound in every good work. As it is written: 'They have freely scattered their gifts to the poor; their righteousness endures forever.'"

"I pray "child" will be generous and willing to share, laying up treasures for himself/herself as a firm foundation for the coming age." 1 Tim. 6:18-19

Day 5

Notes: _____

_____

_____

_____

_____

_____

_____

_____

_____

_____

_____

_____

_____

HONESTY

Proverbs 11:1-3 (TLB) "The Lord hates cheating and delights in honesty. ² Proud men end in shame, but the meek become wise.³ A good man is guided by his honesty; the evil man is destroyed by his dishonesty."

"I pray _"child"_ will always be totally honest with God, Dad, Mom and themselves. May integrity and honesty be their virtue and their protection." Ps. 25:21

Day 6

Notes: _____

_____

_____

_____

_____

_____

_____

_____

_____

_____

_____

_____

_____

_____

LOVE

1 John 4:10-12 This is love: not that we loved God, but that he loved us and sent his Son as an atoning sacrifice for our sins. Dear friends, since God so loved us, we also ought to love one another. No one has ever seen God; but if we love one another, God lives in us and his love is made complete in us. Romans 5:8 tells us God loved us so much that he sacrificed his son for us while we were still sinners. We also can be loving and kind even when others are being hateful and selfish.

"Lord, I pray _"child"_ will learn to live a life of love, through the Spirit who dwells in him/her." (Gal. 5:25; Eph. 5:2)

Day 7

Notes: _____

_____

_____

_____

_____

_____

_____

_____

_____

_____

_____

_____

JOY

It is an internal gladness, it is not happiness that depends on our circumstances and our moods; which has to do with our emotions or station in life. This joy is something that is constant; it is from within us because He lives within. One can have the same joy in terrible circumstance that they would have when all is well, the same attitude of being on the mountain top when they are in the valley. 2 Corinthians 8:2 In the midst of a very severe trial, their overflowing joy and their extreme poverty welled up in rich generosity.

"I pray *"child"* will follow your will and your ways and experience great joy. May my child be filled with the joy given by the Holy Spirit." (1 Thess. 1:6)

Day 8

Notes: _____

_____

_____

_____

_____

_____

_____

_____

_____

_____

_____

_____

_____

PEACEFUL

John 14:27 Peace I leave with you; my peace I give you. I do not give to you as the world gives. Do not let your hearts be troubled and do not be afraid. Does enjoying God's perfect peace mean that you'll never feel the effects of the storms raging around you? Hardly. But His peace is complete, adequate, and sufficient for anything you face. Keep in mind three keys to experiencing sustained peace: Focus on God. --- Trust Him. ---Meditate on His Word.

"I pray _"child"_ will grow up to become a peace-maker. Father, let my child 'make every effort to do what leads to peace" Rom. 14:19

Day 9

Notes: _____

_____

_____

_____

_____

_____

_____

_____

_____

_____

_____

_____

_____

PATIENCE

When defined as "waiting without complaint," patience might seem to be a morally insignificant trait. What's so virtuous about not complaining? In itself, not complaining carries no particular virtue. Suppose a person awaits the arrival of a friend from out of town, and she spends the time happily reading or watching television. We wouldn't say that, simply because she's not complaining, she exhibits patience in this case. Something else must be required to make one's lack of complaint virtuous. That something is *discomfort*. It's because a circumstance is uncomfortable for someone that we find her refusal to complain remarkable and thus regard her as patient.

"Lord, I pray *"child"* will have patience in all he/she does, and help run with perseverance the race you marked out for him/her." (Heb. 12:1)

Day 10

Notes: _____

_____

_____

_____

_____

_____

_____

_____

_____

_____

_____

_____

_____

Kindness

It is a personal quality that enables an individual to be sensitive to the needs of others and to take personal action to endeavor to meet those needs. It is more than being nice and agreeable. It is a quality of one's being, not just a matter of a person's behavior! This makes it a personal virtue and not just an action or a personal gift that is given to someone.

"I pray _"child"_ will be sensitive to the needs of others. Help him/her to treat their siblings better than their best friend...   ...In Jesus name, Amen."

Day 11

Notes: _____

_____

_____

_____

_____

_____

_____

_____

_____

_____

_____

_____

_____

_____

GENTLENESS

Gentleness is possibly the most misunderstood value. Many people think of gentleness as being weak, timid, or passive. This is not the biblical understanding of gentleness. The biblical understanding of gentleness is like that of a trained 2000 pound Belgium horse, it's strength under control. *Gentleness is strength under control.*

"I pray "child" will be very strong during challenging times and completely in control...   ...In Jesus name, Amen."

Day 12

Notes: _____

_____

_____

_____

_____

_____

_____

_____

_____

_____

_____

_____

_____

Faithfulness

Proverbs 3:3-4 Let love and faithfulness never leave you; bind them around your neck, write them on the tablet of your heart. Then you will win favor and a good name in the sight of God and man. "It is only a faithful person who truly believes that God sovereignly controls his circumstances. We take our circumstances for granted, saying God is in control, but not really believing it. We act as if the things that happen were completely controlled by people. To be faithful in every circumstance means that we have only one loyalty, or object of our faith— the Lord Jesus Christ." ---Oswald Chambers

"I pray love and faithfulness never leave _"child"_, but bind these twin virtues around his/her neck and write them on the tablet of his/her heart...   ...In Jesus name, Amen."

Day 13

Notes: _____

_____

_____

_____

_____

_____

_____

_____

_____

_____

_____

_____

_____

_____

GOODNESS

God's goodness in His people avoids sexual immorality, impurity, greediness, all disobedience, and fruitless deeds of darkness. On the contrary, God's children live as children of light and seek to please the Lord, "for the fruit of the light consists in all goodness, righteousness and truth" (Ephesians 5:9) Here Paul clearly parallels righteousness and truth with goodness. Finally he calls for us to be filled with the Spirit, blessing God, blessing others, and submitting to one another in the fear of Christ. ---Roger D. Cotton

"I pray "child" will avoid immorality and disobedience. Fill him/her with goodness...   ...In Jesus name, Amen."

Day 14

Notes: _____

_____

_____

_____

_____

_____

_____

_____

_____

_____

_____

_____

_____

_____

SELF-CONTROL

Paul says that Christians exercise self-control like the Greek athletes, only our goal is eternal, not temporal. "Everyone who competes in the games exercises self-control in all things. They then do it to receive a perishable wreath, but we an imperishable" (1 Corinthians 9:25). So he says, "I pommel my body and subdue it" (1 Corinthians 9:27). Self-control is saying no to sinful desires, even when it hurts. But the Christian way of self-control is NOT "Just say no!" The problem is with the word "just." You don't just say no. You say no in a certain way: You say no by faith in the superior power and pleasure of Christ. --- John Piper

"I pray _"child"_ will be able to pass up short-term approval in order to gain long-term respect. Father, help my child not to be like many others around them, but let them be alert and self-controlled in all they do." (1 Thess. 5:6)

Day 15

Notes: _____

_____

_____

_____

_____

_____

_____

_____

_____

_____

_____

_____

_____

RESPECT

Respecting everyone means believers should be especially conscious that God has created all people in His image, regardless of whether they believe in Christ. Therefore, we should show them proper respect and honor because their souls are of more value than all the wealth in the world. **Pray for those in authority over you. Set the example for the people around you.** Show others what submitting to authority for the right reasons is supposed to look like. Don't participate in back-biting, gossiping, or criticizing your bosses or others in authority. There is nothing wrong with having constructive conversations, but there is a fine line between offering your opinion and becoming disrespectful.

"I Pray *"child"* will have respect for self, others, and authority. Grant that my child may show proper respect to everyone, as Your Word commands." (1 Pet. 2:17)

Day 16

Notes: _____

_____

_____

_____

_____

_____

_____

_____

_____

_____

_____

_____

_____

_____

FORGIVENESS

As we receive forgiveness from God, we must give it to others who hurt us. We cannot hold grudges or seek revenge. We are to trust God for justice and forgive the person who offended us. That does not mean we must forget the offense, however; usually that's beyond our power. Forgiveness means releasing the other from blame, leaving the event in God's hands, and moving on.

"I pray _"child"_ will be quick to forgive those who hurt him/her. Help my child know your forgiveness and always pass it on to others."

Day 17

Notes: _____

_____

_____

_____

_____

_____

_____

_____

_____

_____

_____

_____

_____

HONOR

Paul commands us to "be devoted to one another in brotherly love. Honor one another above yourselves" (Romans 12:10). Honoring others, however, goes against our natural instinct, which is to honor and value ourselves. It is only by being filled with humility by the power of the Holy Spirit that we can esteem and honor our fellow man more than ourselves. All true believers are to honor God and His Son, Jesus Christ, through our acknowledgement and confession that He is the one and only God (Exodus 20:3; John 14:6; Romans 10:9).

"I pray _"child"_ will always show honor to you Lord. Help him/her to show honor in every day actions to their father, mother, siblings and everyone else......In Jesus name, Amen."

Day 18

Notes: _____

_____

_____

_____

_____

_____

_____

_____

_____

_____

_____

_____

_____

STEWARDSHIP

The word, stewardship, simply means to manage someone else's property. For the Christian, as Scripture proclaims everything belongs to God, we manage the property of our Lord. Since everything belongs to Christ, we need to have the attitude and view that our things are His things, our stuff is His stuff, that all we could have now, all we have lost, all we will have, is His, including our very bodies and spiritual gifts.

"I pray _"child"_ will know everything belongs to the Lord. Help him/her understand they are caretakers of relationships, money, their stuff and their environment...   ...In Jesus name, Amen."

Day 19

Notes: _____

_____

_____

_____

_____

_____

_____

_____

_____

_____

_____

_____

_____

_____

TENDERHEARTED

"What an excellent thing, then, is a "tender heart." What delight it gives unto the Lord. Why certainly, for it is the product of His own handiwork. By nature the heart of fallen man is very far from being "tender" toward God, for that is what was denoted in the case of Josiah. No, sad to say, it is the very opposite: so far as the Lord is concerned, the heart of every descendant of Adam is hard, callous, stubborn and defiant. Before it can become tender, a miracle of grace needs to be wrought upon it.

"I pray _"child"_ is tenderhearted toward all things Godly. Help him/her understand the miracle of your grace and show grace to others...   ...In Jesus name, Amen.

Day 20

Notes: _____

_____

_____

_____

_____

_____

_____

_____

_____

_____

_____

_____

_____

COMMUNICATION

There are five important areas of communication in your life. First, in your daily communication with God as you hear from him through his word and talk to him in your prayers. We also hear from God when we listen to our Christian elders who have walked with him longer. The second priority in communication is with our spouse. The next area is the daily dialog we have with our children. Finally our work associates and our friends. Our words give encouragement and hope. When we share about the saving knowledge of Jesus Christ, our words bring eternal life. ---Greg C. Gunn

"I pray _"child"_ will become a great communicator of your word and your love to all people he/she comes in contact with...   ...In Jesus name, Amen."

Day 21

Notes: _____

_____

_____

_____

_____

_____

_____

_____

_____

_____

_____

_____

_____

RESPONSIBILITY

Dependability, Reliability & Trustworthiness are all part of the act of carrying out prescribed roles and duties without supervision in home, school, community and society. Responsibility is a force that binds you to your obligations. Being responsible refers to our ability to make decisions that serve our own interests and the interests of others. We first need to be responsible for ourselves before we can be responsible for others. Responsible people look to the long-term goals, and not always what is easy and provides immediate satisfaction.

"I pray _"child"_ will carry out their commitments and do the best he/she can to be responsible for himself/herself... ...In Jesus name, Amen."

Day 22

Notes: _____

_____

_____

_____

_____

_____

_____

_____

_____

_____

_____

_____

_____

TRADITIONS

Traditions are important because they contain our best knowledge collected over the years. **They provide a sense of comfort.** Because traditions are familiar, you know what to expect because the tradition has been repeated over time. There is no surprise or anything new, you have fond memories of the last time you participated and you feel a sense of security. **They bring people closer together.** The holidays give families a reason to come together and celebrate. Even families fraught with interpersonal issues may put their grievances aside for a short time to honor the tradition.

"I pray *"child"* will understand and appreciate the value of our family traditions. Help him/her pass your word on to future generations through traditions...   ...In Jesus name, Amen."

Day 23

Notes: _____

_____

_____

_____

_____

_____

_____

_____

_____

_____

_____

_____

_____

GRACIOUS

Be attentive to what people say. Respond, without interruption. You always have time. You own the time in which you live. You grant it to others without obligation. That is the gift of being gracious. The return — the payback, if you will — is the reputation you will quickly earn, the curiosity of others, the sense that people want to be in the room with you. The gracious man does not dwell on himself, but you can be confident that your reputation precedes you in everything you do and lingers long after you are finished. People will mark you for it. You will see it in their eyes. People trust the gracious man to care. The return comes in kind. To be gracious towards someone is to be generous in heart; expressing unmerited or undeserved favor.

"I pray _"child"_ will have great manners and a gracious spirit. Help him/her develop a great reputation in order to influence people for your glory... ...In Jesus name, Amen."

Day 24

Notes: _____

_____

_____

_____

_____

_____

_____

_____

_____

_____

_____

_____

_____

MERCIFUL

What the Bible promises is not only that God shows mercy to people, but that people can -- *must* -- show mercy to each other. Grudges and getting even are a normal part of the world scene, but they have no place in the life of someone who has enjoyed the mercy of God. The Bible promises blessing for people who can mirror God's mercy. It promises something else for those who refuse. "God blesses those who are merciful, for they will be shown mercy." Matthew 5:7 "There will be no mercy for you if you have not been merciful to others. But if you have been merciful, then God's mercy toward you will win out over his judgment against you." James 2:13

"I pray *"child"* will always know your mercy and become a person who shows mercy to others. May my children always "be merciful, as [their] Father in merciful." Luke 6:36

Day 25

Notes: _____

_____

_____

_____

_____

_____

_____

_____

_____

_____

_____

_____

_____

Compassionate

The meaning of compassion is **to recognize the suffering of others, then take action to help.** The meaning of compassion can be expressed in many ways. The Bible defines the meaning of compassion in several ways. We are to "speak up for those who cannot speak for themselves … defend the rights of the poor and needy" (Proverbs 31:8-9, NIV). We do this by taking action instead of just talking about helping others: "Dear children, let us not love with words or tongue but with actions and in truth" (1 John 3:18, NIV).

"I pray _"child"_ will be able to recognize hurting people and take action to help. Lord, please clothe my child with the virtue of compassion." Col. 3:12

Day 26

Notes: _____

_____

_____

_____

_____

_____

_____

_____

_____

_____

_____

_____

_____

THOUGHTFUL

Thoughtfulness considers others, and gives attention and care to their feelings first. It helps us take the load and focus off ourselves, so as to be able to see the needs around us. It is a form of love that seeks to uplift and do good whenever possible. It is the opposite of selfishness, yet, it does not cause us to neglect ourselves because that would be unkind to God's child-you! It is especially appreciated when it is not expected. Being thoughtful will not allow schedules to take priority over people.

"I pray _"child"_ will be thoughtful of others and care about the feelings of others first. I ask this especially in our family...   ...In Jesus name, Amen."

Day 27

Notes: _____

_____

_____

_____

_____

_____

_____

_____

_____

_____

_____

_____

_____

WORK

The Bible speaks extensively about work and its importance. Rather than viewing it as "a necessary evil," the Scriptures assert God ordained work as one of the purposes for mankind. It also points out hard work can and should be recognized and rewarded. **Work is designed to provide for our livelihoods.** We all have needs – food, shelter, clothing, transportation, and many more. Throughout human history, work has been the primary means for satisfying those needs. *"For even when we were with you, we gave you this rule: 'If a man will not work, he shall not eat'"* (2 Thessalonians 3:10).

"I pray _"child"_ will learn to value work and to work hard with all his/her heart, always working for the Lord and not for men."(Col. 3:23)

Day 28

Notes: _____

_____

_____

_____

_____

_____

_____

_____

_____

_____

_____

_____

_____

Commitment

"To Have and To Hold." Find a way to renew your marriage vows. If you were married in a religious setting, consider visiting the same house of worship and pondering your marriage vows. Wherever you were married, you can plan a special occasion, such as an anniversary, to renew your vows. You might invite a few friends or family members to witness the occasion and hold an informal reception afterwards. Even if you don't take the time to officially renew your vows, make a habit of verbally announcing the commitment you have to each other. It is very important to tell your kids you love your spouse and are committed. Studies show children go further, faster when their parents are committed to each other.

"I pray _"child"_ knows my commitment to our family and becomes a person of commitment in their future family, career and ministry...   ...In Jesus name, Amen."

Day 29

Notes: _____

_____

_____

_____

_____

_____

_____

_____

_____

_____

_____

_____

_____

HUMILITY

The core of every great marriage or family starts with humility on the part of someone. There are many ways to humble ourselves. 1. Look for the best in other family members. 2. Give sincere complements to others. 3. Be quick to admit your mistakes. 4. Be first to apologize during or after an argument. 5. Know and admit your limitations. 6. Be a servant to others. 7. Keep a learning mindset and 8. Always give God credit for everything good.

"I pray *"child"* has the ability to humble himself/herself when needed...   ...In Jesus name, Amen."

Day 30

Notes: _____

_____

_____

_____

_____

_____

_____

_____

_____

_____

_____

_____

_____

TRUST

Do your kids trust you? If you make a promise to a family member, follow through with it. Make a promise that's feasible, and choose your words carefully. If you are put in a position where you have to break the promise, tell the family member as soon as you can. Ask your family members if you have broken trust with them. Ask them if you ever made a promise you did not follow through on. Are you giving your spouse any reason to miss-trust you? Ask is there is anything you are doing that feels untrustworthy. Immediately address the issue and go overboard to make sure trust is established in that area.

"I pray _"child"_ will grow up to be a trustworthy adult. Help him/her know the value of trust and how important it is to build and keep trust in relationships... ...In Jesus name, Amen."

Day 31

Make Your Own Customized Values Calendar with this List of 168 Core Values:

Abundance – A great or plentiful amount

Acceptance – Favorable reception or belief in something

Accomplishment – Doing or finishing something successfully

Accountability – Obligation or willingness to accept responsibility and be answerable for ones actions

Accuracy – Conformity to fact. Precision; exactness.

Achievement – The act of accomplishing or finishing

Adaptable – The ability to modify behavior to fit changing situations

Adventure – Inclination to undertake new and daring enterprises

Allegiance – Loyalty or the obligation of loyalty

Altruism – Unselfish concern for the welfare of others

Ambition – An eager or strong desire for achievement and the willingness to strive for its attainment

Appreciation – Recognizing the quality, value or significance of people and things

Articulacy – Expressing oneself easily in clear and effective language

Assertiveness – Respectfully standing up for ones beliefs and thoughts

Aspiration – A strong or persistent desire for high achievement

Assiduous – Unceasing; persistent; diligent

Authenticity – The quality or condition of being trustworthy or genuine

Autonomy – The condition or quality of being independent

Aware – Informed, alert, knowledgeable and sophisticated

Balance – A state of equilibrium between the key components of life

Benevolence – An inclination to perform kind, charitable acts

Bold – Beyond the usual limits of conventional thought or action

Brilliance – Exceptional clarity and agility of intellect or invention

Calmness – Serenity; tranquility; peace

Camaraderie – Goodwill and lighthearted rapport between or among friends

Caring – Feeling and exhibiting concern and empathy for others

Challenge – The desire to test of one's abilities or resources in a demanding but stimulating undertakings

Changeability – The ability to modify or adapt to differing circumstances

Charity – Generosity toward others or toward humanity

Chastity – The condition of being of virtuous character

Cheerful – The quality of being cheerful and dispelling gloom

Citizenship – Exercising the duties rights, and privileges of being a citizen

Class – Excellence or elegance, in dress, design, or behaviour

Clear thinking – Acting intelligently without mental confusion

Collaboration – To work cooperatively especially in a joint intellectual effort

Commitment – Being bound emotionally or intellectually to a course of action or to another person or persons

Community – Sharing, participation, and fellowship with others

Compassion – Deep awareness of the suffering of others and the wish to relieve it

Competence – The state or quality of being adequately or well qualified

Competitive – To strive to do something better than someone else or yourself

Composure – Maintaining a tranquil or calm state of mind

Concern – Regard for or interest in someone or something

Conscientious – The trait of being painstaking and careful

Consideration– Thoughtful or sympathetic regard or respect for others

Consistency – Reliability or uniformity of successive results or events

Constancy – Steadfastness in purpose

Cooperation – The willing association and interaction of a group of people to accomplish a goal

Courage – The state or quality of mind or spirit that enables one to face danger or fear with confidence and resolution

Courtesy – Civility; consideration for others

Creativity – the generation of new ideas or concepts

Credibility – Worth y of belief or confidence. Trustworthy.

Decency – Conformity to prevailing standards of propriety or modesty

Decisive – Characterized by decision and firmness; resolute.

Dedication – Selfless devotion of energy or time

Democracy – The principles of social equality and respect for the individual within a community

Dependability – The trait of being reliable

Determination – Firmness of will, strength, purpose of character

Discipline – Act in accordance with rules

Diversity - A point of respect in which things differ; variety

Easygoing – Relaxed or informal in attitude or standards

Education – Obtaining or developing knowledge or skill through a learning process

Efficiency – The quality of producing an effect or result with a reasonable degree of effort to energy expended

Empathy – Identification with and understanding of another's situation, feelings, and motives.

Encouragement – The act of incitement to action or to practice

Equality – The right of different groups of people to receive the same treatment

Equity – The state, quality, or ideal of being just, impartial, and fair

Excellence – State of possessing good qualities to a high degree

Fairness – Consistent with rules, logic, or ethics

Faith – Confident belief in the truth, value, or trustworthiness of a person, idea, or thing

Faithful – Adhering firmly and devotedly to someone or something that elicits or demands one's fidelity

Fidelity – Faithfulness; loyalty or devotion

Flexibility – Responsive to change

Focus – Able to concentrate intently

Forgiveness – The willingness to stop blaming or being angry with someone

Fortitude – The strength or firmness of mind that enables a person to face danger, pain or despondency with stoic resolve

Freedom – The power to determine action without restraint

Friendship – A relationship between people based on mutual esteem and goodwill

Fun – Enjoyment and playfulness

Generosity – Liberality in giving or willingness to give

Gentle – The quality of being mild and docile

Genuine – Not spurious or counterfeit

Giving – To present voluntarily and without expecting compensation

Goodness – Morally right, or admirable because of kind, thoughtful, or honest behavior

Goodwill – A friendly attitude in which you wish that good things happen to people

Gracious – **pleasantly kind, benevolent, and courteous.**

Gratitude – A feeling of thankfulness and appreciation

Hardworking – Industrious and tireless

Helpful – The property of providing useful assistance or friendliness evidence by a kindly and helpful disposition

Honesty – Fairness and straightforwardness of conduct

Honor – Principled uprightness of character; personal integrity

Hope – The feeling that something desired can be had or will happen

Humility – Feeling that you have no special importance that makes you better than others

Independent – Freedom from the control, influence, support, or the like, of others.

Individuality – The particular character, or aggregate of qualities, that distinguishes one person from others

Industrious – The characteristic of regularly working hard

Influence – The ability to move or impel a person to some action

Ingenuity – Cleverly Inventive skill or imagination; Resourceful

Initiative – Ability to begin or to follow through energetically with a plan or task

Insightful – Characterized by or displaying insight; perceptive

Integrity – Strict adherence to moral values and principles

Intelligence – The capacity for learning, reasoning and understanding

Joy – Intense or exultant happiness

Justice – Conformity to moral rightness in action or attitude

Kindness – The quality or state of being beneficent

Law-abiding – Abiding by the encoded rules of society

Leadership – The act or instance of leading; guidance; direction

Learning – The act or process of acquiring knowledge or skill

Liberty – The right and power to act, believe, or express oneself in a manner of one's own choosing.

Love – A feeling of intense desire and attraction toward a person or idea

Loyalty – A feeling or attitude of devotion, attachment and affection.

Mindful – Being attentive, aware, or careful

Moderation – Having neither too little or too much of anything

Obedience – Compliance with that which is required; subjection to rightful restraint or control.

Open-minded – Receptive to new ideas. Unprejudiced; unbigoted; impartial

Open – Unreserved, candid, or frank. To disclose, reveal, or divulge

Opportunity – Favorable or advantageous circumstance or combination of circumstances

Optimism – A bright, hopeful view and expectation of the best possible outcome

Patience – The ability to accept delay, suffering, or annoyance without complaint or anger

Peace – Freedom from war or violence

Perseverance – Steady persistence in adhering to a course of action, a belief, or a purpose

Personal Growth – The acquisition of knowledge, skills, and experience for the purpose of enhancing individual performance and self-perception

Philanthropy – An altruistic concern for human welfare and advancement,

Practicality – Mindful of results, usefulness, advantages or disadvantages of an action or procedure. Matter-of-fact

Professionalism – The standing, practice, or methods of a professional, as distinguished from an amateur.

Promise-keeping – Keeping your word that that you will certainly do something

Prudence – Doing something right because it is the right thing to do

Punctuality – Adherence to the exact time of a commitment or event

Purity – Moral goodness

Reason – The ability to think and make good judgments

Recognition – An acceptance as true or valid

Reconciliation – Enabling two people or groups adjust the way they think about divergent ideas or positions so they can accept both

Reliability – Consistent performance upon which you can depend or trust

Repentance – Remorse or contrition for past conduct

Resilience – The ability to rebound quickly from misfortune or change

Resourceful – The ability to act effectively or imaginatively, especially in difficult situations

Respect – Showing regard or consideration for.

Responsibility – That for which someone is responsible or answerable

Results-oriented – Maintain focus on obtaining a notable or successful result or response; be effective

Righteous – The state of being morally upright; without guilt or sin

Sacrifice – To give up something for something else considered more important

Sagacity – Acuteness of mental discernment and soundness of judgment

Self-control – Control of personal emotions, desires, or actions by one's own will

Sensitivity – Awareness of the needs and emotions of others

Serenity – Calmness of mind and evenness of temper

Sharing – To allow others to participate in, use, enjoy, or experience jointly or in turns

Significance – The quality of being significant or having a meaning

Simplicity – Freedom from complexity and intricacy. Absence of pretentiousness.

Sincerity – Genuineness, honesty, and freedom from duplicity

Sobriety – Habitual freedom from inordinate passion or overheated imagination; calmness; coolness; seriousness

Stamina – The physical or mental strength to do something for a long time

Stewardship – The careful conducting, supervising, or managing of something

Strength – Moral power, firmness, or courage

Supportive – Furnishing support or assistance

Thoughtful – The tendency to anticipate needs or wishes

Tolerance – Recognizing and respecting the beliefs or practices of others

Tradition – The customary or characteristic method or manner

Tranquility – A state of calm and peacefulness

Trustworthy – The trait of deserving confidence

Understanding – Knowing how something works or a positive, truthful relationship between people

Unique – Not typical; unusual

Unity – Oneness of mind and feeling among a number of persons; Concord, harmony or agreement

Virtue – Doing something right because it is the good thing to do

Vitality – Exuberant physical strength or mental vigor.

Warmth The quality of being intimate and attached

Willing – Cheerfully consenting or ready

Wisdom – The ability to make good judgments based on what you have learned from your experience

Witty – Amusingly clever in perception and expression

Zeal – Fervor for a person, cause, or object; eager desire or endeavor; enthusiastic diligence;